AF576278

CHARLOTTE

A Touch of Gold

To Charlotte,
the end of our rainbow.

CHARLOTTE
A Touch of Gold

Photographs by Bill Gleasner
Text by Diana Gleasner

First printing, 1983.

ISBN 0-914788-74-4 / LC 83-048036

Design by Steve Galit Associates

Printed by China Color Printing Co., Inc.
Taipei, Taiwan, R.O.C.

Published by The East Woods Press
Fast & McMillan Publishers, Inc.
429 East Blvd.
Charlotte, NC 28203

SHERATON

Charlotte: A Touch of Gold *Diana Gleasner*

This blossoming city in a forest of trees looks around in quiet astonishment. A heritage of feisty independence has given her presence—a natural bearing of grace and purpose. Having transcended a turbulent youth and uncertain adolescence, Charlotte now finds herself radiant with beauty.

Sparkling with future promise, she remains sensitive to her surroundings. It is not an accident that both pale pink dogwood and sky-grazing towers of commerce sprout from her fertile red soil.

Charlotte, with quickening pace, is coming into her own. She is more than the crossroads of the Carolinas, much more than a handsome and tranquil place to settle.

She is a touch of gold glowing in the Southern sunshine.

A Land Abundantly Blessed

The richness was always here . . . buffalo bellowing across a sea of prairie grass, bear crashing through wild pea vines, the clear and swift Catawba River funneling mountain streams toward the Atlantic.

The Catawba Indians, "people of the river," prized this territory, so abundantly blessed with virgin forests, fresh water, fish and game. While the men hunted and fought off marauding tribes, women wove baskets and fashioned pots from red clay dug from the river banks. Unfortunately, white traders brought "strong drink" and even stronger disease. The combination proved a formidable foe for the courageous Catawbas, whose nation was eventually decimated as a result.

The Indians had followed animal trails rather than beat back the underbrush. Their main path, the way taken by white settlers journeying south, soon became the major route through the Piedmont. By the mid-1700s, the trickle of traffic along the Catawba Trading Path developed into a steady stream.

They came to see if the tales were true. Was the climate mild, the land really fruitful much of the year? Could the birds be so plentiful they actually broke the tree limbs with their weight? There was only one way to find out. They packed their goods on sturdy horses and followed the ancient trail south.

Scotch-Irish Settlers Build a Town

Thomas Spratt was the first to bring a wagon into the Carolina wilderness. Thomas Polk, with an eye on Spratt's lovely daughter Susannah, was not far behind. They, like so many who followed, were Scotch-Irish from Pennsylvania. The specter of harsh frontier life was no determent to these stout-hearted Presbyterians who prized freedom and opportunity far above the comforts of city life.

Tom Polk was a stalwart man of action. He married Susannah and built her a house at the intersection of the Catawba Trading Path and another wagon trail (corner of Trade and Tryon streets). With a couple of neighbors he purchased 360 acres which had been part of a land grant given to Lord Selwyn by the King of England. Polk looked around at the scattered log houses of the tiny settlement and envisioned an honest-to-goodness town.

The Polks' home was in Mecklenburg, a county established in 1762. Tom and his neighbors took it upon themselves to erect a log courthouse where the two paths crossed. First they pushed for a charter for their village and then, using the courthouse as the trump card, campaigned to be county seat. Polk, energetically fenagling his way through the intricacies of government, eventually got his way. In 1768 the N.C. Assembly granted the charter, commending the location for its "healthfulness" and "as a convenient place for trade." One hundred acres were divided into half-acre house lots and Charlotte Town became a reality.

Charlotte was named for the new bride of King George III of England just as Mecklenburg County was named for her German birthplace. No doubt the town fathers hoped honoring the Queen might smooth the way for the isolated community which had already had run-ins with tax-collecting agents of the Crown. Besides, the name had a pleasant ring to it, and the Queen was greatly admired. As a 17-year-old princess, she had already demonstrated a social consciousness. Upset by constant wars waged by the King of Prussia, she begged him to stop the carnage. Her carefully phrased letter included the admission that it might seem ". . . unbecoming of my sex, in this age of vicious refinement, to feel for one's country, to lament the horrors of war or to wish for peace." Yes, she was a worthy woman, and Charlotte a name the growing town could wear with pride.

British Soldiers Stir Up a Hornet's Nest

The men and women drawn to the wilds of North Carolina had strong convictions and unwavering values. Ardent believers in God, education, hard work and freedom, they took a very dim view of English meddling.

These pioneers faced enough problems without paying a new British tax every time they turned around. Reverend Alexander Craighead fanned the embers of their dissatisfaction into a bonfire of resolve. His fiery rhetoric was a weekly spur to action. How could they obey God when they were squeezed in the vice of British tyranny?

Reverend Craighead, who had been booted out of Maryland and Pennsylvania for preaching against the Crown, was welcomed as pastor of both Rocky River and nearby Sugaw Creek Church. His eloquent exhortations in favor of political and religious liberty made perfect sense to his parishioners.

Tom Polk was also fed up with British oppression. As commander of the county militia, he called for two representatives from each militia district to gather at the courthouse on May 19, 1775. It was time to take matters into their own hands.

These community leaders were mostly churchmen from the area's seven Presbyterian churches. Their anti-British fervor was fever-pitched even before they heard a courier rein his galloping horse to a dusty stop outside the courthouse. The news could not have been more ominous. One month before, the courier said, the British had fired on colonists at Lexington, Massachusetts.

The horrified gathering was quick to draw conclusions. With British protection withdrawn, they owed not a shred of allegiance to the King. If one colony was attacked, they were all in danger.

On May 20, 1775, a year before the American Declaration of Independence, the people of this backwoods community ignited a beacon of liberty. Their Mecklenburg Declaration of Independence severed all connections with the Crown. They further resolved to be self-governing, a radical, perhaps disastrous, move. They knew that, should England triumph, they might end up hanging from the gallows. The Mecklenburgers solemnly pledged "their lives, their fortunes and their most sacred honor."

The colonists believed they would not, could not, fail. Their cause was just, their will indomitable. The crowd rallied around their leaders. With tumultuous glee, they tossed their hats into the air in celebration. It would not be easy, but this victorious moment should be savored. The people were united in their vision of a better tomorrow, gathering strength for the storm to come. It was exhilarating to be at the forefront of events that would certainly change their world.

Unfortunately, the Mecklenburg Declaration was never read at the Second Continental Congress. North Carolina delegates who carried it proudly to Philadelphia were told it was too early for such strong sentiments. Hope of resolving the colonies' difficulties with England was still alive. (Although historians have gone to a great deal of trouble to substantiate the facts surrounding the Mecklenburg Declaration of Independence, a few still question its existence.)

Five years after the Mecklenburg Declaration of Independence, the town saw its words translated into action. The American Revolution was not going well for the British. General Cornwallis had taken Charleston but the cost had been great. Charlotte Town, a community of only 20 homes, seemed a likely place for his troops to rest and gather supplies.

Cornwallis severely underestimated the hostility of the

populace. A handful of men welcomed the British with a flurry of rifle fire. The skirmish was the first in a series of trials that would plague Cornwallis in Charlotte.

The General set up headquarters in Tom Polk's house and issued a proclamation commanding the citizenry to turn in their arms and stay peacefully at home. They did neither. This was Charlotte's chance to show its mettle. British foraging parties met resistance everywhere. Sharpshooting Americans seemed to lurk behind every bush. Farmers drove their livestock deep into the woods and burned their barns rather than feed the enemy. Communications were seriously disrupted. Cornwallis, without being able to send or receive messages, found himself isolated in hostile territory. He wrote that Charlotte was "an agreeable village" but a "damned hornet's nest of rebellion." (A hornet's nest, symbol of this zeal, graces the city seal.)

The British, low on food and enduring constant harassment, suffered mightily from their stay in Charlotte. In two short weeks they would lose a major battle at Kings Mountain. A year later Cornwallis surrendered to General Washington at Yorktown.

Gold!

Charlotte's post-war years were sunny ones. George Washington, the young republic's first president, paid a social call, merchants prospered and farmers reaped bumper crops from their fertile land. The invention of the cotton gin profoundly affected the area's economy as more and more acreage was devoted to the lucrative cash crop. With wealth came enough leisure for social and artistic pursuits. Charlotte was growing in sophistication as well as numbers.

Who could have imagined the riches to come! Certainly not young Conrad Reed, who in 1799 stumbled on a 17-pound gold nugget while wading in a stream on his farm near Concord. The family used the heavy rock as a doorstop. Later, after learning it was gold, Conrad's father spent a lot of time getting his feet wet. One lucky day his stream yielded a 28-pound nugget, the largest ever found in this country.

Word spread and soon farmers were hurrying through chores so they could search for gold before daylight waned. An epidemic of gold fever gripped the region. Almost overnight Charlotte became the mining capital of the country. The downtown area was honeycombed with the shafts of nearly 100 mines. A great mix of people, from hopeful prospectors to skilled engineers, converged on the city from near and far. Business—all kinds of business—boomed.

Much mining was done in shallow open pits or by panning in steams for nuggets referred to as "branch gold." Some mines were highly productive despite the crude techniques used to recover the precious metal. Primitive machinery pulverized the ore, leaving much that was low-grade as waste. The city put these tailings to good use: Charlotte's streets were literally paved with gold.

Getting the gold coined presented a real problem since the mint was located in Philadelphia, a long, rough trip by horse, wagon or stage. After much petitioning, Congress finally authorized the building of a Charlotte Branch Mint in 1835. More than $5,000,000 in one dollar, quarter and half eagle coins were turned out before operations were shut down in 1861. By that time many afflicted with gold fever had long since moved on to richer lodes as they joined the California Gold Rush of 1849.

Bonnets, Leeches and Gander Pulling

As the first half of the nineteenth century slipped into the past, an agrarian lifestyle went with it. Those "good, old days" were not entirely idyllic. Bonneted women hid from the sun lest they become "speckled as a hen's egg." No self-respecting female would think of seeking employment outside the home. Doctors regularly bled their patients for a variety of ills or prescribed the application of leeches which were sold at the corner drugstore. Educational theory was fairly simple. A teacher asked only to be given a boy and a book, offering to furnish discipline in the form of a hickory branch. Dueling was considered a civilized way of resolving arguments and, for sport, there was always gander pulling. As they galloped by a goose that hung by its feet, riders would try to be the first to pull off its head.

Life Turned Inside Out

With the coming of the railroads in 1852, Charlotte's growth potential increased dramatically. Within a decade, however, progress came to a crashing halt as the nation was ripped apart by Civil War. After being threatened by Federal Forces, the

Confederate Naval Ordnance facility at Norfolk was moved inland to Charlotte. The Charlotte Mint functioned as a hospital for wounded soldiers and as local headquarters for the Confederacy. Life turned inside out as men and money were sacrificed for the struggle. Town records were hidden in the country, bank vaults emptied and their contents buried in the woods. Even the church bell was melted down to make weapons. Though its spirit and resources were severely depleted, the city survived four years of war physically unscathed. Charlotte emerged from the interminable Reconstruction period with hopes for a much brighter future.

The populace, having endured the rigors of war, learned to accept change with comparative equanimity. Not surprising was the response of a man awakened by his hysterical family to find the earthquake of 1886 jolting his home. "Go back to your beds," he said with irritation. "Don't you know the judgment day is not coming in the night?"

The Turn of the Century

The turn of the century found more than 18,000 people in Charlotte taking in stride such miracles as the telephone and the first automobile. They even had a new-fangled trolley system installed by Thomas Edison's electric company and owned by Edward Dilworth Latta, a man who envisioned a great future for this town.

In 1890 Mr. Latta dreamed up Charlotte's first suburb and named it Dilworth. He bought a thousand-acre tract of rural land, divided it into lots and curving streets, and ran his trolley to it. The last stop on the line was Latta Park, a gloriously green refuge where hardworking city folk might wile away their leisure hours. Charlotteans came in droves to attend theater and sporting events or to picnic by the lily pond.

Ease of access has been a prime factor in the city's growth since Thomas Spratt drove his wagon down the Catawba Trading Path. In the mid-1800s the fact that the Trade and Tryon intersection was wide enough for an eight-mule cotton wagon to turn around made the town a logical marketplace. Later the railroad's arrival revitalized a slumping economy. Since city fathers were keenly aware of transportation's importance, they gave top priority to the construction of a sound network of arteries to link the city with the rest of America.

These highways and Charlotte's ideal location between the population centers of the Northeast and the agricultural areas of the South proved to be a fruitful combination. In the first decade after the turn of the century, Southern Power Company (now Duke Power) set about harnessing the Catawba River. A plentiful labor supply and ample electric power at economical rates helped the area shift swiftly from a producer of cotton to a thriving textile center. As the farm economy dwindled drastically, Charlotte became an important base for distribution as well as manufacturing. Diversified industry attracted an ever-widening pool of trades, businesses and professions, adding muscle to the economy. In 1909 Charlotte watched her first skyscraper, the old Independence Building, climb cloudward. By 1910 she was (and still is) the largest city in North Carolina.

Being a key participant in the industrialization of the South gave Charlotte big ideas. Patriotism was at high tide when she put in a successful bid for a World War I army training camp. The fact that 60,000 troops would make the camp larger than the city itself wasn't a problem, but an unusually harsh winter was. Interminable rains and snows turned Camp Greene into a swamp of oozing red mud. Worse yet, many young men died during a severe influenza epidemic before they ever reached the battlefields of Europe.

The people of Charlotte were genuinely concerned about the strangers in their midst. They invited them home for dinner, often forming lasting friendships. Camp Greene provided a boost which went well beyond mere economic stimulus. Many who passed through Charlotte in uniform remembered this warm hospitality and returned after the war to make their homes here.

Hanging On

The Great Depression ravaged the citizens of Charlotte as it did those of every city in the United States. The name of the game was survival and to this end some people sold apples on street corners or joined their neighbors in soup lines. Because labor was cheap, a few gold mines reopened briefly when the government increased the price of gold from $20.67 to $35 an ounce. But for the most part, the thirties were grim years of hanging on and hoping for better times ahead.

As the country was again swept into the maelstrom of international conflict, the city was able to make a significant contribution to the World War II effort. An airport expansion accommodated increased air traffic. Charlotte was the chosen site for the U.S. Navy shell-loading plant and for a huge Quartermaster Depot which processed supplies for many southeastern army bases. The additional activity of World War II further stimulated an economic recovery already underway in Charlotte.

Postwar Charlotte was soon a burgeoning metropolis basking in the sunshine of prosperity and growth. So much needed doing, she could hardly wait to roll up her sleeves and get started. During the fifties and the sixties, ambitious redevelopments replaced slums. Thanks to a carefully thought-out plan, desegregation was accomplished peaceably. The city's first enclosed shopping center, Charlottetown Mall, was built in 1959.

City limits were expanded time and again to embrace the sprawling suburbs. Here and there a towering high rise created a skyline of promise. Charlotte was definitely on the move.

The Best Kept Secret

Now in the eighth decade of the twentieth century, Charlotte's growth shows no sign of slowing. On the contrary, she has racked up some rather impressive statistics on which to build. As the sunbelt's major financial center, her banking resources exceed those of any other city between Philadelphia and Dallas. She is the transportation center of the Southeast, and the largest and one of the fastest growing cities between Washington and Atlanta.

While all these superlatives cast a golden hue over the Queen City, they do not begin to tell her story. Those guiding the city's growth never actively sought to be number one in size, wealth or prestige. Rather, they were striving for a balanced growth that would not in any way diminish the qualities that make Charlotte so livable.

Charlotte's council-manager form of government, adopted in 1929, has drawn national attention because of the unusually smooth interaction between the city manager and the council. Elections are partisan, with the mayor and 11-member council elected in November of odd-numbered years. Four of the council members are at large and seven represent districts.

The success of local government is as evident in wide, shady streets banked with azaleas as it is in the glistening rebirth of uptown. Ever since Trade Street evolved from the Catawba Trading Path, the city has been, without apology, a center of commerce. While other cities grabbed for short-term glitter, Charlotte burnished a long-range plan. Her controlled expansion is rooted firmly in a diversified economy of finance, transportation, industry, communications and services. Implementing the plan took patience and a steady grip on the helm, but the results are apparent.

A middle-sized city in the heart of the sixth largest urban region in the country, Charlotte is committed to development. In this urban region, known as Metrolina, 1.3 million people live in 12 counties in North Carolina and South Carolina. Charlotte, as Metrolina's central business district, could scarcely avoid growth. The questions are: how and in what direction?

Conveniently situated between New York and Florida and between the mountains and the coast, Charlotte's location works for her. She attracts people of diverse cultures and interests and in that diversity finds enormous strength and flexibility. Perhaps this explains her ability to blend business and beauty, progress and tradition, bustle and tranquility.

Charlotte basks in an enviable year-round climate with four distinct seasons. Spring's flowering dogwoods and azaleas turn the residential areas into a fairyland of blossoming color. Summer brings warm days and pleasant nights. A long, mild autumn gives everyone plenty of opportunity to appreciate the leaves as they blaze gold and red against a bright blue Carolina sky. Winter always slips a few spring-like days into its brief, brisk visit.

Charlotteans once thought of their hometown as the South's best kept secret. No more. The word is out. Anything the city lacks in a slick image is more than made up in personality. Her people are polite, warmly hospitable and, in a gentle way, proud of their city.

There is much to be proud of. Cultural offerings run the gamut from ballet to puppet shows, from chamber music to Summer Pops Concerts in Freedom Park. An active Opera Association brought the world premiere of "Abelaird and Heloise" to the city. The Charlotte Symphony has been performing for half a century.

Both professional and amateur theater thrive. Playgoers choose from offerings at Spirit Square's intimate NCNB Performance Place, Golden Circle productions at the Mint Museum of Art, touring Broadway shows at Ovens Auditorium and a rich selection of plays and musicals at Charlotte Little Theatre, Children's Theatre and nearby colleges and universities.

The Mint Museum of Art houses the world-famous Delhom Collection of Pottery and Porcelain and one of the Southeast's best exhibits of pre-Columbian pottery. The museum is involved in an expansion program which includes seven new galleries to hold the permanent collection and the recent multi-million dollar gift of art works from the Dalton family of Charlotte. Expansion plans call for three large galleries for outstanding traveling exhibitions from America's major museums.

History buffs tour the Hezekiah Alexander House, the oldest dwelling still standing in Mecklenburg County. Listed in the National

Register of Historic Places, the house is completely refurnished in period pieces. The Mint Museum of History displays artifacts from Charlotte's early days and sponsors a popular annual colonial crafts festival. Fourth Ward, just a few blocks from the city's skyscrapers, makes good use of its historic treasures. Homes in this 200-year-old neighborhood sparkle with restored Victorian splendor.

Spirit Square, Charlotte's center for the arts located in a renovated church, offers lectures, classes and workshops on a myriad of subjects. Neighborhoods host such colorful festivals as the ebullient Springfest in Fourth Ward, Festival-in-the-Park in Freedom Park and Dilworth Jubilee in Latta Park.

Charlotte's newest museum, Discovery Place, is as entertaining as it is educational. At this hands-on museum of science and technology visitors create electricity, meet the resident octopus and stroll through a tropical rain forest.

Mecklenburg County has a long tradition of commitment to academic excellence; the first college in North Carolina was founded in Charlotte in 1771. Today's fine family of colleges and universities includes Davidson College, Johnson C. Smith University, Queens College, U.N.C.-Charlotte, Belmont Abbey and Central Piedmont, the state's largest community college.

Charlotte boasts two newspapers, the Charlotte Observer and the Charlotte News, the Carolinas' largest morning and evening dailies. The Charlotte Observer Marathon, held annually in January, draws national talent as well as legions of local runners and well-wishers.

Sports and recreational pursuits have always been an important part of the leisure scene. Lake Norman, the state's largest man-made lake, is a scant 15 minutes north of the city. With 520 miles of shoreline, this "inland sea" offers unlimited opportunities to boat, sail, fish, swim, waterski and camp. Another convenient destination for aficionados of water sports is Lake Wylie, south of Charlotte. Charlotteans who love surfing and snowskiing don't have far to travel. A wide choice of weekend and vacation get-aways is waiting at the coast and in the mountains a few hours' drive from the city.

Residents make good use of their many parks, pools, tennis courts and golf courses. Elegant country clubs with fine facilities add another dimension to the recreational and social picture.

Avid spectators have two pro teams to cheer for. Carolina Lightnin' Soccer, a member of the Freedom Division of the American Soccer League, and the Charlotte O's baseball team, a Baltimore Oriole Minor League club, attract a loyal and vocal following.

Charlotte Motor Speedway stock car races capture the national spotlight during the World 600 and the National 500. More than a dozen professional racing teams live in the area and fans flock here from all over the country.

A constant stream of visitors enjoys Carowinds, an amusement park straddling the border between North Carolina and South Carolina. Features include all sorts of family fun, a campground and no less than five roller coasters. Top name performers play its Palladium every weekend from spring to fall.

Another widely known area institution is PTL, one of the largest Christian broadcasting networks in the world. The "PTL Club" talk show is carried in all 50 states and in many nations abroad. PTL's 1200-acre complex, Heritage USA, is a Christian retreat and conference center which draws more than 100,000 visitors each year.

The farmers' markets, flea markets, church suppers, parades and barbecues sponsored by various groups are a long-established part of the Charlotte scene. Charlotte also hosts a number of special events including the U.S. Open Jumping Championship, one of the most prestigious stops on the Equestrian Grand Prix Tour.

Conventions and trade shows put the facilities at the Civic Center, the Trade Mart and the Merchandise Mart to frequent good use. The Southern Christmas Show heralds the holiday season and the Southern Living Show's tulips are the first sign of spring.

Meeting Urban and Suburban Needs

As the Tryon Street Transit/Pedestrian Mall takes shape, the uptown area is blending retail, office and convention requirements with residential, recreational and cultural needs. The heart of the city is vibrant with activity.

Charlotte's neighborhoods are flourishing. Community action groups bristle with enthusiasm. Once, long ago, folks were surprised to see a stranger cross Independence Square. Those were the days when everyone knew, and shared a concern for, everyone else.

Today, that spirit of caring has been rekindled as Charlotteans pull together to better their lives.

More and more snowbelt refugees and other seekers of the "good life" are attracted to this clean and friendly city. The population of Mecklenburg County, now more than 400,000, is projected to be 506,000 by 1990. Growth creates challenge as well as opportunity. Charlotte, with more cars per household than any other similar size city in the country, has already begun to improve its public transit system. Increasing numbers of single-person households have encouraged a variety of housing options including townhouses and condominiums. As more people choose to make their homes in the city, there is greater incentive to mix the best features of urban and suburban life. Beauty and safety are as high on the priority list as culture and convenience.

Where is Charlotte headed? The best answers take a long look at where she's been. The original settlers had a sure sense of who they were and why they chose to live here. That knowledge bolstered them through years of rapid-fire transition. Succeeding generations watched in amazement as their tiny crossroads village blossomed into a thriving urban center.

Today, planners are optimistic, and why shouldn't they be? With the confidence of maturity, Charlotte is reaffirming cherished values as she reaches out for a golden tomorrow.

1774

MERCEDES-B

3138
189
American Athletics
2484
421
277

SPRINGFEST
CHARLOTTE

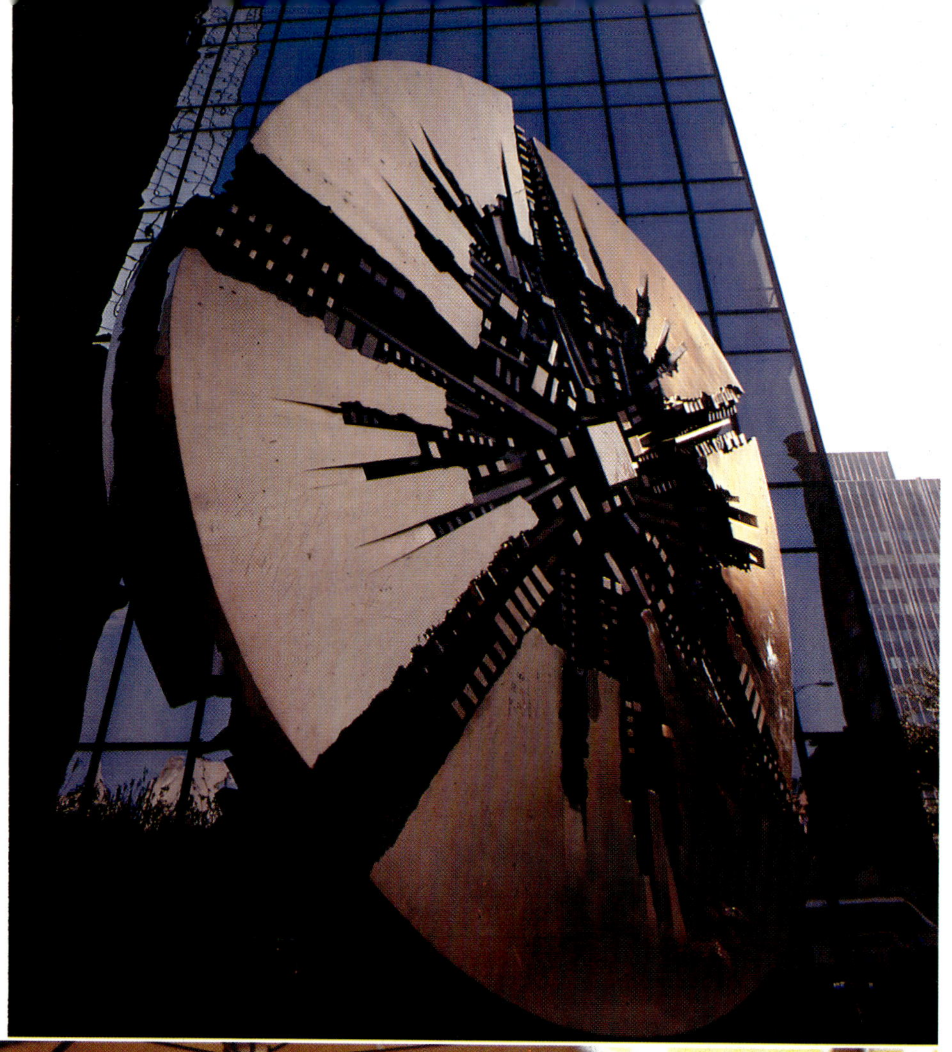

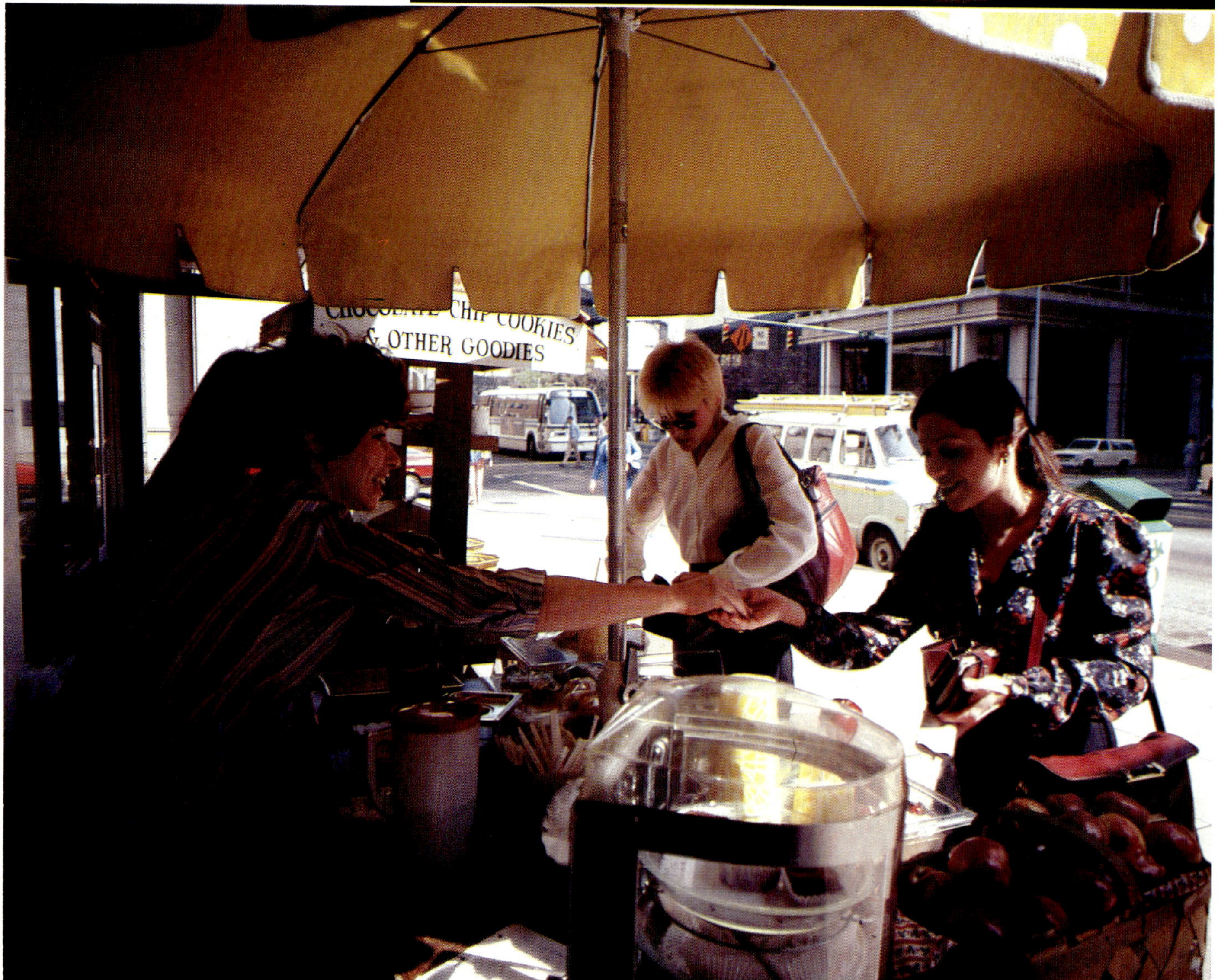
CHOCOLATE CHIP COOKIES
& OTHER GOODIES

OUNTY COURT HOUSE

HARDWARE
KISTLER
Hardware
Since 1928
ONE WAY
SEEDS
Charlotte is cleaning up. It feels good.
KISTLER HARDWARE PARKING CUSTOMERS ONLY 333-4555
ANY TIME
POSITIVELY NO PARKING RESERVED SIDE
KISTLER HARDWARE

JUNE MUSIC
UPTOWN PROMOTION
NCNB24

NUT HOUSE

23706
59031

CHARL

OTT

Charlotte